Unpredictable Waters

ZARA ALI

BookLeaf Publishing

India | USA | UK

Presentation by *BookLeaf Publishing*

Web: www.bookleafpub.com

E-mail: info@bookleafpub.com

ISBN: 9789357446372

First edition 2022

DEDICATION

To you dear reader, and to me

ACKNOWLEDGE MENT

First of all, thank you dear reader for taking the time to read this book. If you have bought this as a physical copy then thank you once again. Secondly, Book Leaf Publishing gave me this opportunity, thank you a million. It has been a journey albeit a very short one but I have learnt so much. I would like to thank my family and friends who did not know this was going to be published. Just to be clear, this does not include every single one of you, those who are dear to me and have supported me know who they are. In the next book I will be super specific so that there is no mistake or room for assumptions. And last but not least, I would like to thank the three most inspirational Bob's I have come across in my life and at different stages. Bob the builder, for showing me perseverance because 'Can we fix it?' 'Yes we can!', Bob Ross because 'there are no mistakes, just happy accidents' and Bob Proctor because 'if you can hold it in your mind, you can hold it in your hand.'
I am holding this in my hand.
Until next time.

PREFACE

If you are reading this, then I must commend you, because I must confess that I very rarely read the preface in books. Writing a poem a day for 21 days was a challenge that I almost thought that I would fail. Nevertheless I persevered.

The theme of water to others is strange, and of that there is no doubt. But in reality, this little book is about mental health. I have often described my depression as the ocean, always constant and always so unpredictable. I found it easier to explain the bad days in that way but also I found much strength in those dark and murky waters, because the ocean has always brought me peace. It is a strange thing to describe, to associate it with something so volatile and yet find it to be a source of comfort. So I think that you will find that the ocean is not only a metaphor for my depression but also a metaphor for my capacity to love. And although this is my first official publication, and it is smaller than most, I hope that you can find something for yourself in these words. I leave behind pieces of me to you.

The first poem is dedicated to you.

Unpredictable Waters

I heard someone say
Our mind is an ocean
At times violent
At times suffocating with its current
If it is as they say
Our mind is an ocean
Then I will always wish you calm waters

Skies above

2

When the heavens cry
I am comforted
Knowing the sky suffers too

Teardrops

I gather my tears
My precious diamonds
And bury them in the soil
A piece of me left behind
A piece of me eternal
They seep in and water my plants
At least there will be some use of these droplets
Because no one else sees their worth
Nor feels their weight

Smothering love

5

My love is the ocean
At times turbulent
At times serene
But always vast, endless to the eyes
Constant
Always deeper than the admirer believes
Its depth is unknown
Like the world that resides beneath its surface

My love is the ocean
As beautiful as it is dangerous
Be careful how far you swim
For you may just drown
To those to whom my love was too much to bear
I am sorry if I smothered you

Dream

I had a dream that I stood in a place free of time
It had no power over me
A place where the sky touched the ocean
Surrounding its reflection
A world of blue abandoned
Free of people
Free of noise
A place untouched by humanity
I woke up crying
How I wish I could have stayed there
For it was only a dream that I wished could be a
reality

Winter to spring

I am radiant in winter
For my smile never leaves my lips
Surrounded by the sniffles and groans of
humankind
I cannot help but revel in the bitter cold
My fingers numb
Feet wet from the snow
The winds slash through my body as though I
am their enemy
And perhaps in some ways I am
A single figure smiling in the cold

When I return to the comfort of my home
A sea of warmth hugs me
A hot shower
Comfortable clothes
A fire crackling in the hearth
A hot cup of tea
Ah
Bliss, simple, exquisite bliss

This shall be my routine
My smile shall waver
As the ice melts and spring begins

Remember me

8

My love touches the earth in every drop of rain.
Like the water it flows, vast and endlessly for
you my dear.
Remember me
As vibrant as I once was
I am the gentle breeze that caresses you
Stroking your head as I once did
I have not left you alone my dear
I am the snowflake that melts on the tip of your
nose
A soft kiss
I shall be with you always

Blue

Your ocean eyes
Hungry, relentless
Majestic
And yet, infinitely warm
I am lost in the sea

The night sky
Somber and dazzling
Blanketed with starts
You are a million miles from me

All that is blue
Reminds me of you

Your lips
As your last breath escapes
With a shakiness not meant for someone with
such youth
Hot tears spill over
As those ocean waves hush slowly to stillness
Your world blacks out in front of you
So does mine

Paradox

You bring me such joy
And such pain
You are my umbrella
And my rain

Water

I'm sinking
However, I do not mind
The water has always brought me more comfort
and relief than the humans surrounding me
I feel peace in the rain, the familiar sound of 'pit,
pit, patter' as the drops hit the surface. A familiar
friend, checking in and knocking on my window.
I feel loved when I am at sea, the comforting
sound of the waves crashing against the sand. A
lover, wrapping themselves around me with each
movement, caressing me lazily. Simply
worshipping my body.
I feel relaxed in the shower, the pressured
streams hitting my naked body. A masseuse
massaging my hot damp skin, undoing all my
tension, stress and worry filled knots. Easing me
into a slumber unlike any other.
Its blanket wraps me
My throat burns from the water
My eyes sting
Sometimes I wish I did not wake to see another
day

Kings & Queens of spring

My heart is an ocean frozen
Hidden, who knows what lies beneath the
surface?
Ice so cold
Each of those words you breathed against my
skin
Dented my heart
And like a dam it broke
Your hands were my anchor
Your heart my demise
Your love a summer breeze
That set me alight
Like spring follows winter
You melted me down

Now the water flows freely
The sky is it's ceiling
It knows no bounds
Fearlessly
Unabashedly
You wade through the water
And call it your home

What boils beneath

Eyes fierce
A smile saccharine
A mask so deadly
At first glance
All seems well
But observe the silence
A little more
Something's not quite right
About an expression plastered
No crows feet line those eyes
If you are patient enough
You may just see
A glimpse of what lies beneath
A split second change
A crack in the facade
Like a rubber band
It contracts back into place
So what will you see?
Sends shivers down your spine
A prayer leaves your lips
You find yourself becoming more aware
Following their presence with your eyes
Deep down below
You can see their blood boiling
Like a kettle that is reaching its peak

Their jaws are clamped
However, there is no relief
Keep your distance
When the tide is low
Lightning strikes high
If you are close enough
You'll feel the earth tremble wherever they tread
A masked angel in your presence
Is actually the devil instead

Compulsion

15

Water compels me
I wonder why?
Do I descend from an ancient line of seafarers?
Or is it the memory of my mother's womb that
brought me comfort?
Is it the way the amniotic fluid wrapped around
me and conformed to my shape that I miss?
Is that why, in times of stress and worry, I seek
out bodies of water?
Is that why I relish in the showers from above
and why I feel so lost at the shoreline?
Or perhaps it is simply science
A body craving oxygen of a physical kind.

Spring

16

And if my heart is clay
Will you be the rain to make the garden grow?

Rain

17

I lay in the front yard
Drenched
I closed my eyes
And let the heavens
Cleanse me of my sins
And wash away my sorrow

Just a drop

Jump in the puddles
Dance in the rain
Swim in the ocean
Wash yourself of all pain
Live freely
Forget everything
And do all the little things that bring you joy
Life is too short to live up to the demands and
expectations of society
We are merely a drop in the ocean that is the
universe

Drowning

Your hand keeps me under water
Yet you tell me to swim
Your hand keeps me under water
Yet you wonder aloud, how it is that I am
drowning

Dissociation

Some days I am not myself
When this life has become too much to bear
I escape this reality and place myself at the
shores of a beach
A happy place
A sanctuary
My life carries on unbeknownst to me
I stay for days at a time
When I return my memory leaves me
Sometimes it is merely hours
Other times it is weeks
Whatever time is lost
Is enough to heal the wounds that reopen
It is enough to give me the strength to live for
tomorrow

Let it go

I trudged through life
Collecting my burdens, my grudges and grief
Like rocks in a sack across my shoulders
One by one
An ever growing pile
Until I could no longer bear their weight
At a lake, I broke
Out poured my fears, my insecurities, my
grudges, burdens and grief
I emptied the sack
And let it all go
Not for you
But for me

Catching up

I sip tea while I spill the tea
Such an afternoon of entertainment

Yin & Yang

I was water
You were a flame
Such delicate balance between us
That would otherwise end in pain

You would extinguish me from existence
I would drown you the same
It is such a wonder
How we still remain